an
ALPHABET
of sweets

Merry Christmas
Dan & Barb
We hope that the
recipes are as good
as the art —
Love,
Jackie & Dick

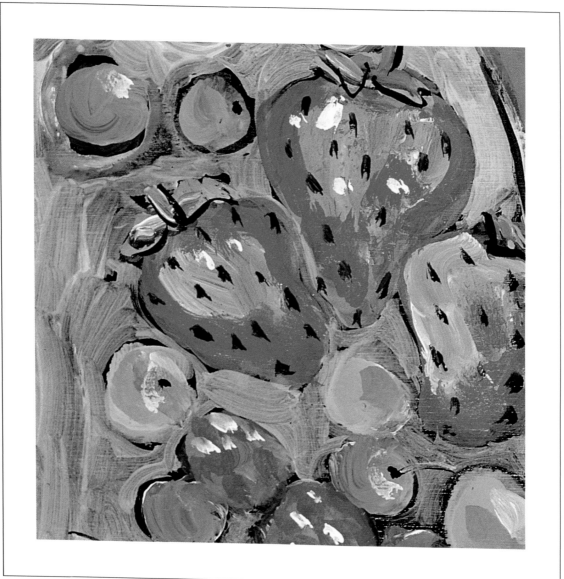

MARCEL DESAULNIERS

an
ALPHABET
of sweets

ILLUSTRATED BY

NANCY GARDNER THOMAS

First published in the United States of America in 1996 by

Rizzoli International Publications, Inc.
300 Park Avenue South
New York, New York 10010

Library of Congress Cataloging-in-Publications Data

Desaulniers, Marcel.
    An alphabet of sweets : 26 confections from the author of Death by
chocolate / Marcel Desaulniers ; illustrations by Nancy Tomas.
        p.   cm.
    ISBN 0-8478-1981-7 (hc)
    1. Confectionary. I. Title.
TX783.D47 1996
    641.8'6—dc20   96-18490
                                    CIP

Designed by Elizabeth Woodson

Printed and bound in Singapore

MARCEL'S DEDICATION
To my wife Connie—for your love, friendship, and vision

NANCY'S DEDICATION
To my daughters Wendel, Hunter, and Laura—for their love and inspiration

Acknowledgments

Very appreciative thanks go to Dan Green, Jon Pierre Peavey, John Curtis, Penny Seu,
and the staff at the Nancy Thomas Gallery
(especially Robert, Tara, Gail, and Mary Lynn for making life easier)

CONTENTS

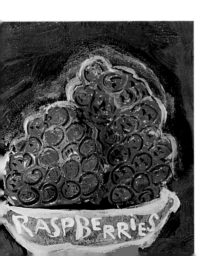

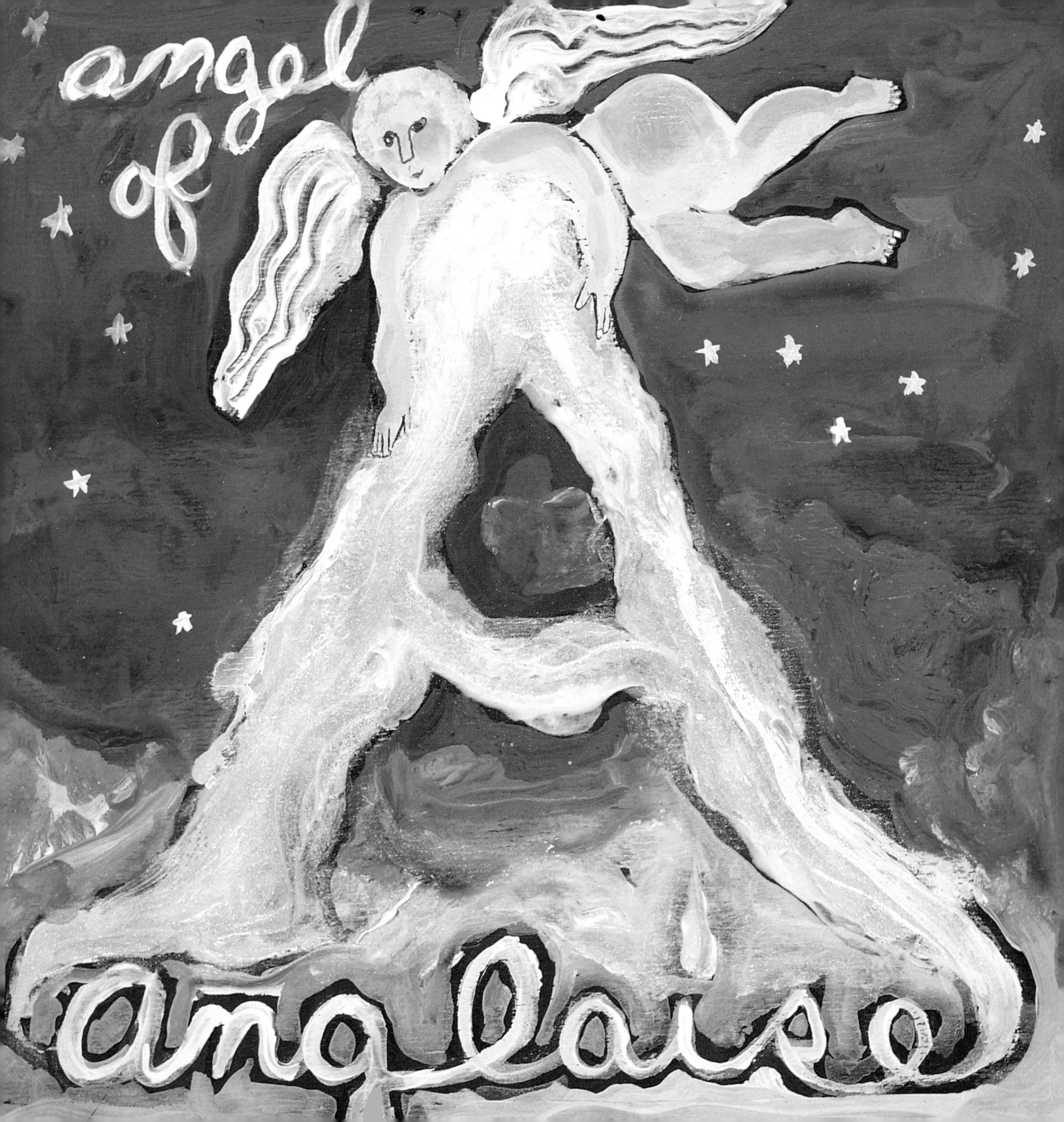
angel of
anglaise

WHITE CHOCOLATE CREME ANGLAISE

As surely as the angels float effortlessly through the heavens, so will this delicate sauce as it flows from your mouth to your tummy.

INGREDIENTS
(Yields 1 1/2 cups)

4 OUNCES WHITE CHOCOLATE, CHOPPED INTO 1/4-INCH PIECES

1 CUP HEAVY CREAM

2 LARGE EGG YOLKS

2 TABLESPOONS GRANULATED SUGAR

This ethereal confection is created by first melting the white chocolate very slowly in the top half of a double boiler over low heat. While the chocolate melts, heat the heavy cream in a saucepan over medium heat and bring to a boil. • It takes a few minutes for the cream to boil, but rather than gazing at the stars, whisk the egg yolks and sugar in a separate bowl for 3 minutes. Carefully pour the boiling cream into the egg yolk and sugar mixture, then stir very gently to combine. Return the mixture to the saucepan and heat over medium-high heat, stirring constantly just until the mixture begins to simmer. Pour the simmering mixture into the bowl with the melted white chocolate, stirring gently to combine. • The *crème anglaise* may be used immediately, perhaps with your favorite chocolate cake. Since heaven can wait, you can also cool the sauce and serve it chilled with freshly picked berries. White Chocolate Crème Anglaise, warm or cool, will make you feel good inside.

UTTERLY BUTTERY BITTERSWEET CHOCOLATE BUTTERCREAM

**You'll feel blessed every time you make this heavenly frosting.
The secret to its success is to melt the chocolate slowly so that it becomes a silky and willing recipient for the remaining ingredients.**

INGREDIENTS
(Yields 3 cups)

4 OUNCES SEMISWEET
CHOCOLATE, CHOPPED INTO
1/4-INCH PIECES

3 OUNCES UNSWEETENED
CHOCOLATE, CHOPPED INTO
1/4-INCH PIECES

3/4 POUNDS UNSALTED BUTTER,
CUT INTO **12** PIECES

1/2 CUP GRANULATED SUGAR

Place both the semisweet and unsweetened chocolate in the top half of a double boiler over, but not touching, simmering water. Use a rubber spatula to gently and constantly stir the chocolate as it slowly melts (while you are thinking delicious thoughts). As soon as the chocolate is smooth, remove it from the heat and set it aside to cool to room temperature (about 78 degrees Fahrenheit). • Place the butter and the sugar in the bowl of an electric mixer fitted with a paddle. Beat the butter on low speed for 1 minute, then on medium speed for 2 minutes. Use a rubber spatula to scrape down the sides of the bowl. Now pick up the pace, and beat the butter mixture on high until light and fluffy, 7 to 8 minutes. Scrape down the paddle and the sides of the bowl. • Add the melted chocolate to the fluffy butter and sugar and beat on medium for 1 minute. Adjust the mixer speed to high and beat for 1 minute until thoroughly combined and lustrous in color. After you swipe one delectable taste (well, maybe two) you'll still have enough buttercream to lavishly frost one double layer chocolate cake or 5 to 6 dozen cup-cakes (party time).

11

CARAMEL PEANUT CHOCOLATE CHUNK ICE CREAM

**If being carried away on a wave of caramel is a dream come true, read on.
Caramel is simple to make and scrumptious to eat. But be forewarned: a stream of hot caramel
can be as treacherous as a turbulent sea, since hot liquefied sugar can burn skin.
Therefore, please prepare the caramel for this ice cream carefully.**

INGREDIENTS
(Yields 2 quarts)

1 1/2 CUPS GRANULATED SUGAR

1/4 TEASPOON FRESH
LEMON JUICE

1 3/4 CUPS HALF-AND-HALF

1 3/4 CUPS WHOLE MILK

6 LARGE EGG YOLKS

1 CUP TOASTED UNSALTED
PEANUTS

6 OUNCES SEMISWEET
CHOCOLATE, CHOPPED INTO
1/4-INCH CHUNKS

Place 1 cup sugar and the lemon juice in a 3-quart saucepan and stir until the sugar resembles moist sand. Place the pan over medium heat, stirring constantly as the mixture liquifies and turns light brown. At this point, remove the pan from the heat (resist the temptation to stick your finger into the sugar; it's too darn hot). Immediately add 1/2 cup half-and-half and stir to combine. Transfer the caramel to a large bowl and allow it to cool to room temperature. Heat the remaining 1 1/4 cups half-and-half and the milk in a 3-quart saucepan over medium-high heat and bring to a boil. While the cream is heating, whisk the egg yolks and the remaining 1/2 cup sugar in a large bowl until slightly thickened and lemon-colored. Pour the boiling cream and milk mixture into the beaten egg yolks and stir to combine.

• Return the mixture to the saucepan and heat it over medium-high heat, stirring constantly until it barely simmers; do not boil. Remove the egg yolk mixture from the heat and immediately add to the prepared caramel, whisking to combine. • Place the bowl in ice water and stir it constantly until the mixture is cold. Freeze the cold mixture in an ice cream freezer following the manufacturer's instructions. Transfer the semifrozen ice cream to a plastic container, then fold in the peanuts and chocolate. Securely cover the container, then place it in the freezer for several hours before serving. Serve within 3 to 4 days. That's an order from the Captain!

DEVILISH DIAMONDS

Diamonds have always been a girl's best friend. But then we added a little pepper, and the Duchess—who likes things spicy and devilish—claimed them for her own. The itty-bitty amount of pepper will tickle the tongue, but it won't leave anyone reaching for a handkerchief.

INGREDIENTS
(Yields 16 diamonds)

8½ TABLESPOONS UNSALTED BUTTER

8 OUNCES UNSWEETENED CHOCOLATE, CHOPPED INTO ¼-INCH PIECES

2¼ CUPS GRANULATED SUGAR

4 LARGE EGGS

1 TEASPOON PURE VANILLA EXTRACT

1½ CUPS ALL-PURPOSE FLOUR

1 TEASPOON FRESHLY GROUND BLACK PEPPER

ICE CREAM (OPTIONAL)

Mine your diamonds by first preheating the oven to 350 degrees Fahrenheit. Line the bottom and long sides of a 9- by 13- by 2-inch nonstick cake pan with a single sheet of parchment paper. Coat the paper with ½ tablespoon butter; set aside. • Melt the chocolate and remaining butter in the top half of a double boiler over medium heat, stirring until completely melted and smoothly combined. Remove the mixture from the heat and set it aside.

• Place 2 cups sugar, the eggs, and vanilla in the bowl of an electric mixer fitted with a paddle, and beat on high for 2 minutes; use a rubber spatula to scrape down the sides of the bowl. Beat the mixture on high for 1 additional minute, add the melted chocolate and butter, and beat on medium for 1 minute. Add the flour and mix on low speed until it is incorporated, about 1 minute. Remove the bowl from the mixer and use the rubber spatula to finish mixing the batter until smooth and thoroughly combined. • Transfer the batter to the cake pan, spreading evenly. Sprinkle the ground pepper, then the remaining ¼ cup sugar, evenly over the top of the batter and bake it in the center of the oven until a toothpick inserted in the center of the cake comes out clean, 38 to 40 minutes. Remove the cake from the oven and allow it to cool in the pan at room temperature for 1 hour. • Now here's the Duchess' favorite part: creating more Diamonds than you can sneeze at. Remove the cake from the pan, then use a serrated slicer to cut the cake lengthwise into 4 (2-inch-wide) strips. Then cut each strip at a diagonal into 4 equally sized diamond shapes, and you have more than a dozen magnificent chocolate jewels. Allow the Duchess a regal indulgence by proffering a big bowl of ice cream along with the Devilish Diamonds.

FROZEN DOUBLE ESPRESSO CREAM

Espresso has its devotees and detractors. To some, it is a desperately bitter brew; to others, a precious elixir. The latter are the privileged few, because for them an assertive yet charismatic dessert awaits.

INGREDIENTS
(Yields 4 servings)

1 1/4 CUPS HALF-AND-HALF

1/2 CUP GRANULATED SUGAR

1/4 CUP FRESHLY GROUND
ESPRESSO BEANS

4 LARGE EGG YOLKS

1 TABLESPOON CORNSTARCH

1 TEASPOON MINCED
LEMON ZEST

1 1/2 CUPS HEAVY CREAM

To create it for your own empire, first heat the half-and-half, 1/4 cup sugar, and the ground espresso beans in a 3-quart saucepan over medium-high heat. Bring to a boil, then immediately strain the mixture through several layers of cheesecloth into a medium-size bowl (and enjoy the rich aroma of the espresso). • In a separate medium-size bowl, whisk together the egg yolks, cornstarch, and remaining 1/4 cup sugar until slightly thickened and lemon-colored. Add the strained half-and-half mixture and the lemon zest to the egg mixture, and whisk gently to combine. Pour the mixture into a clean 3-quart saucepan and heat over medium heat, stirring constantly until the mixture comes to a boil and becomes thick yet smooth. Remove from the heat, transfer to a large bowl, then place the bowl in ice water and stir constantly until cold. Cover the bowl with plastic wrap and refrigerate for 30 minutes. • In a well-chilled bowl, whisk the heavy cream until stiff peaks form. Add about one-quarter of the whipped cream to the chilled espresso mixture and whisk gently to combine. Use a rubber spatula to fold the remaining whipped cream into the espresso mixture until smooth. Divide the mixture into 4 (8-ounce) coffee cups, cover loosely with plastic wrap, and freeze for 2 hours before serving. • Like an official decree, the Frozen Double Espresso Cream is best served immediately. If you prefer something richer (perhaps you're a cousin of the Empress?), then top the dessert with some additional whipped cream and a few shavings of chocolate. That should keep the citizens happy.

ROCKY ROAD FUDGE

This Rocky Road fudge is anything but a bumpy ride. Although loaded with chocolate, pecans, and marshmallows, it's a sweet journey from start to pleasing finish.

INGREDIENTS
(Yields 2 pounds)

2 CUPS TIGHTLY PACKED LIGHT BROWN SUGAR

¾ CUP HEAVY CREAM

2 OUNCES UNSWEETENED CHOCOLATE, CHOPPED INTO ¼-INCH PIECES

4 TABLESPOONS UNSALTED BUTTER

1 CUP TOASTED PECANS

3 CUPS MINIATURE MARSHMALLOWS

To get the show on the road, heat the sugar and cream in a 3-quart sauce-pan over medium heat. When the mixture is hot, stir to dissolve the sugar. Bring to a boil, then lower the heat and allow the mixture to simmer, stirring frequently, for 15 minutes. Remove from the heat, add the chocolate, and use a whisk to stir gently until smooth and thoroughly combined. A word of fatherly advice: it's too hot to taste yet, so don't. • Transfer the mixture to a large bowl; add the butter and stir until thoroughly combined. Now add the pecans and use a rubber spatula to incorporate the pecans evenly through the mixture. Add the mini-marshmallows and use the rubber spatula to quickly mix in the marshmallows until they are evenly distributed into the mixture but not melted. (It's okay to taste now!) • Line an 8- by 8- by 2-inch cake pan with plastic wrap. Pour the fudge mixture into the pan and spread it evenly to the edges; cool at room temperature for 30 minutes, then refrigerate. Now for the tough part: wait 2 hours or so for the fudge to set in the fridge. If this feels like penance, find solace in knowing that it won't be long before you can sink your teeth into some mighty fabulous fudge.

YIN YANG GANACHE

**Ganache is mysterious. In its most basic form, ganache is the harmonious union of boiling cream and chopped chocolate, stirred until smooth.
The metaphysical results can be used as a sauce or icing when warm; as a truffle mixture, for piped cake decorations, or as a base for a bed of nails when chilled.**

INGREDIENTS
(Yields 3 1/2 cups)

8 OUNCES SEMISWEET CHOCOLATE, CHOPPED INTO 1/4-INCH PIECES

12 OUNCES WHITE CHOCOLATE, CHOPPED INTO 1/4-INCH PIECES

1 1/2 CUPS HEAVY CREAM

Start by placing the chopped chocolates into separate medium-size bowls. Heat the heavy cream in a saucepan over medium-high heat; bring to a boil, keeping a close watch to guard the cream against boiling over the sides of the saucepan (what an unforgivable mess). • Pour half the boiling cream over the dark chocolate and the remaining half over the white chocolate. Stir each with a whisk until smooth (stir the white chocolate mixture first if the moon is in the seventh house; otherwise, it doesn't make any difference). Simultaneously pour both ganaches into a larger serving bowl, creating a swirled appearance. • The Guru likes to find the largest, most luscious strawberries possible and individually dip them into the ganache, eating one after the other. If you're feeling more pedestrian, use the ganache as described above.

HAZELNUT HONEY PIE

If you have bees in your bonnet, then dash to the kitchen to make your own Honey Pies.

INGREDIENTS
(Yields 4 small pies)

2 CUPS TOASTED HAZELNUTS

1 CUP ALL-PURPOSE FLOUR

10 TABLESPOONS
UNSALTED BUTTER

4 TABLESPOONS ICE WATER

1/2 CUP TIGHTLY PACKED
LIGHT BROWN SUGAR

1/2 CUP HONEY

2 LARGE EGGS

Start exercising your prerogative by preheating the oven to 325 degrees Fahrenheit. Coarsely chop 1 cup of hazelnuts; set the nuts aside. Place the remaining hazelnuts and the flour in the bowl of a food processor fitted with a metal blade; process for 10 seconds. Transfer the hazelnut/flour mixture to a medium-size bowl, and add 4 tablespoons of butter, using a fork to "cut" the butter into the flour and nuts. Add the ice water, 1 tablespoon at a time, and continue to use the fork to mix the ingredients until it forms a loose ball. Don't be bashful; use your hands to finish mixing the dough (but don't overwork it) and form it into a smooth round ball. • Divide the dough into 4 (4½-inch-diameter and 1-inch-deep) round, solid-bottomed, plain-sided tartlette molds. Use your hands to press the dough into the bottom and against the sides of each mold; set the molds aside. • Place the remaining 6 tablespoons of butter, the brown sugar, and the honey in the bowl of an electric mixer fitted with a paddle. Beat on medium speed for 2 minutes, then scrape down the sides of the bowl. Add the eggs and beat on medium for 2 more minutes. Remove the bowl from the mixer, add the coarsely chopped nuts, and then use a rubber spatula to mix the batter until smooth and thoroughly combined. • Divide the batter among the dough-lined tartlette molds. Place the molds on a baking sheet and bake in the center of the oven until golden brown, about 30 minutes. Remove your little Hazelnut Honey Pies from the oven and allow to cool before serving. If a swarm has gathered in your hive, then serve them a glass of milk along with the Honey Pies. The first forkful of this miraculous manna will have them droning with pleasure.

HIGH PRIESTESS

OLD-FASHIONED PEACHES AND SWEET CREAM ICE CREAM

No other fruit is more evocative of summertime than a peach. Certainly the perfume of a ripe peach, subtle and sweet as a lullaby, inspires cooks to orchestrate confections with this most dulcet fruit. If you are prepared to entertain many a tongue, follow along.

INGREDIENTS
(Yields 2 quarts)

1½ POUNDS RIPE PEACHES, UNPEELED, PITTED, AND CHOPPED INTO ⅛-INCH PIECES

1 CUP GRANULATED SUGAR

2 CUPS HEAVY CREAM

2 CUPS WHOLE MILK

6 LARGE EGG YOLKS

1 TEASPOON PURE VANILLA EXTRACT

First, in a medium-size bowl combine the chopped peaches with ½ cup sugar, cover with plastic wrap, and refrigerate until needed. Heat the cream, milk, and ¼ cup sugar in a 3-quart saucepan over medium-high heat. When hot, stir to dissolve the sugar, then bring to a boil. • While the cream is heating, whisk the egg yolks and the remaining sugar in a large bowl until slightly thickened and lemon-colored. Pour the boiling cream and milk mixture into the egg yolks and stir to combine. Return the mixture to the saucepan and heat over medium-high heat, stirring constantly, until it barely simmers. Remove from the heat, add the vanilla extract, and place the pan in a large bowl of ice water, stirring constantly until the mixture is cold.

 • Freeze the cold mixture in an ice cream freezer following the manufacturer's instructions. Transfer the semifrozen ice cream to a plastic container, then use a rubber spatula to fold in the peaches and their juices. (True impresarios delight themselves first, so taste it now.) Securely cover the container, then place in the freezer for several hours before serving. The peach ice cream is best served within 2 days. Try slicing additional ripe peaches, sprinkle them with sugar, and serve them with the ice cream for a culinary symphony. Ya, Ya, Ya—*Yum.*

PEANUT BUTTER AND JELLY COOKIES

Ever met anyone who didn't like peanut butter and jelly? If so, that person may need a comedian to lighten up a world devoid of one of the tastiest and ticklish combinations to entertain the palate. If you are a peanut butter and jelly fan, don't fool around any longer.

INGREDIENTS
(Yields 2 dozen cookies)

2 CUPS ALL-PURPOSE FLOUR

1 TEASPOON BAKING SODA

1 CUP TIGHTLY PACKED
LIGHT BROWN SUGAR

1 CUP CRUNCHY PEANUT BUTTER

8 TABLESPOONS (¼ POUND)
UNSALTED BUTTER

2 LARGE EGGS

1 TEASPOON PURE
VANILLA EXTRACT

1 CUP OF YOUR FAVORITE JELLY
(OR JAM)

CHOPPED PEANUTS (OPTIONAL)

Get in your kitchen and preheat your oven to 375 degrees Fahrenheit. While the oven heats, sift together the flour and baking soda onto wax paper.
• Place the light brown sugar, peanut butter, and unsalted butter in the bowl of an electric mixer fitted with a paddle, and beat on medium speed for 2 minutes. Add the eggs and the vanilla, and beat on medium for 1 more minute. Use a rubber spatula to scrape down the sides of the bowl. Add the sifted dry ingredients to the sugar and butter mixture and mix on low speed (that's *low* speed or you will certainly make a mess) until the mixture becomes a firm dough, about 30 seconds. • Remove the dough from the bowl. Portion 24 heaping tablespoons of dough onto a clean dry surface. Use your hands to form each portion into a rough textured ball (most feet are simply too big for this task). Place the balls about 1 inch apart on 2 non-stick baking sheets, then use the back of a teaspoon to form a deep indentation in the center of each ball. Bake the cookies in the center of the oven for 10 minutes, until they are very lightly browned. Remove the cookies from the oven, and while they are still hot, place a slightly heaping teaspoon of jelly in the center of each. Serve immediately while still warm, or at room temperature (they can be kept at room temperature in a tightly sealed plastic container for a couple of days). For a mischievous touch, sprinkle chopped peanuts over the jelly. These cookies are so yummy, you'll do cartwheels.

KRISPY KIWI KRINGLE

Don't step on my brown suede fruit! The Kiwi fruit's peculiar brown and fuzzy exterior belies its luscious, and lustrously green flesh.
If you want to rock the dessert boat then roll into the kitchen and get started.

INGREDIENTS
(Yields 4 to 8 servings)

1½ CUPS ALL-PURPOSE FLOUR

5 TABLESPOONS UNSALTED BUTTER

5 TABLESPOONS ICE WATER

1 LARGE EGG YOLK

¾ CUP GRANULATED SUGAR

2 WHOLE KIWI FRUIT PEELED AND CUT INTO ⅛-INCH SLICES

WHIPPED CREAM

Place the flour and butter in the bowl of an electric mixer fitted with a paddle. Mix on medium speed for 1 minute until the butter is "cut into" the flour and the mixture develops a coarse texture; do not overmix. In a small bowl whisk together the ice water and the egg yolk, then add the mixture to the bowl. Mix on low speed for about 30 seconds until a loose dough forms. Remove the dough from the mixer and form it into a smooth round ball. Wrap in plastic wrap and refrigerate for 1 hour. • Preheat the oven to 325 degrees Fahrenheit. Remove and reserve ¼ cup of sugar. Lightly sprinkle a clean, dry work surface with some of the remaining ½ cup sugar. Now it's really time to roll. Unwrap the dough and place it on the work surface. Using a rolling pin, roll the dough into a 12- by 6-inch rectangle. Lightly sprinkle the dough with sugar, then fold in half lengthwise. Once again roll the dough into a 12- by 6-inch rectangle. Arrange the kiwi fruit slices, overlapping slightly, lengthwise down the center of the dough in two side-by-side rows, leaving a 1-inch border on each length and a ⅛-inch border on each end. Fold the sides of the dough toward the center, leaving a 2-inch-wide "window" for the kiwi fruit. • Sprinkle the reserved ¼ cup of sugar over the dough and exposed kiwi fruit slices. Use a spatula to transfer the pastry to a nonstick baking sheet, and bake in the center of the oven for 30 to 32 minutes until golden brown. Remove from the oven and allow to cool for a few minutes before cutting into desired portions. Don't miss a beat—serve immediately with lots of whipped cream.

LOLLIE'S LICORICE LIP SMACKERS

It's not polite to stick your tongue out, unless you are dangling for a Lip Smacker. In that case, proper etiquette would call for you to start these dazzling suckers right away.

INGREDIENTS
(Yields 8 Lip Smackers)

1 CUP GRANULATED SUGAR

1/4 TEASPOON
CREAM OF TARTAR

1/4 CUP WATER

2 TEASPOONS LICORICE OR
ANISE EXTRACT

1 TEASPOON RED FOOD COLOR

8 POPSICLE STICKS

Heat the sugar, cream of tartar, and water in a 1½-quart saucepan over medium heat. When hot, stir to dissolve the sugar, and bring the mixture to a boil. Boil, stirring frequently, for 10 to 12 minutes until the mixture takes on a light honey color. Remove the saucepan from the heat. Add the extract and the red food color, and use a whisk to stir gently until thoroughly combined. • One at a time, dip 1 inch of one end of each popsicle stick into the hot sugar mixture. Place the dipped sticks onto 2 nonstick baking sheets, 4 sticks per sheet, leaving lots of room between sticks. Pour 1 tablespoon of sugar mixture over the dipped ends of each stick, allowing the mixture to flow into a round lollipoplike shape. • Allow the Lip Smackers to harden at room temperature. Of course, by then, many willing lips will be smack dab in the kitchen to try them out. Any remaining smackers should be wrapped with plastic wrap and refrigerated or frozen in a sealed plastic container. With Lip Smackers like these, who needs Kisses?

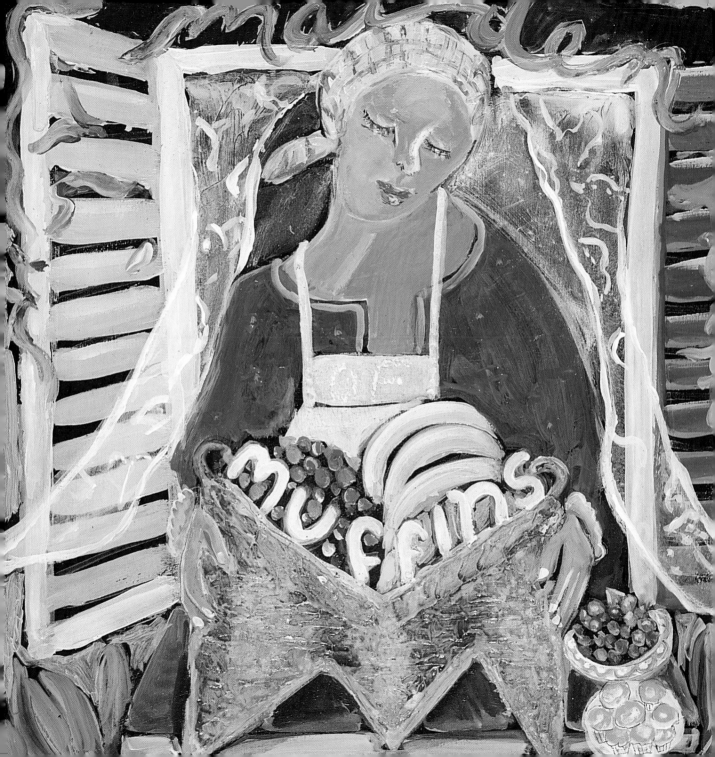

MERRY MAÑANA BERRY BANANA MINI-MUFFINS

**The maiden is merry because she can enjoy one of these diminutive muffins today and *mañana*.
These charming bites, each overflowing with blueberries and bananas,
are perfect for anyone not ready to make a commitment to an oversized, overbearing muffin.**

INGREDIENTS
(Yields 3 dozen)

2 CUPS ALL-PURPOSE FLOUR

½ CUP TIGHTLY PACKED LIGHT BROWN SUGAR

1 TABLESPOON BAKING SODA

2 MEDIUM RIPE BANANAS, PEELED

1 CUP BUTTERMILK

2 LARGE EGG WHITES

8 TABLESPOONS (¼ POUND) UNSALTED BUTTER, MELTED

1 CUP BLUEBERRIES, STEMMED AND WASHED

1 CUP CHOPPED TOASTED WALNUTS (OPTIONAL)

Begin the wooing process by preheating the oven to 400 degrees Fahrenheit. Combine the flour, brown sugar, and baking soda in a large bowl. Smash the bananas to a lumpy consistency in a medium-size bowl, using the back side of a dinner fork, then add the buttermilk and egg whites, and whisk to combine. Now add the butter and stir gently to combine (pretty mushy stuff, but even the most resolute maiden could fall for them in the end). • Pour the mushy banana mixture into the bowl with the dry ingredients and use a rubber spatula to quickly fold (4 to 6 folds) the mixture together. Add the blueberries and gently stir to incorporate the berries into the batter. Evenly divide the mixture—about 1 slightly heaping tablespoon per muffin—among 36 miniature nonstick muffin cups. For added flavor and texture, sprinkle chopped toasted walnuts over the muffin batter in each cup. Bake in the center of the oven until a toothpick inserted in the center comes out clean, 10 to 12 minutes. Allow to cool to room temperature before removing the muffins from the pans. Don't leave anyone out; make a batch for any combination of maidens, mistresses, and even masters.

NUTTY NOUGAT NUGGETS

You don't need a wealth of time or a personal fortune to make this confection. But your mouth will feel as rich as Fort Knox when you eat one of these golden nuggets.

INGREDIENTS
(Yields 32 nuggets)

1 CUP GRANULATED SUGAR

3/4 CUP LIGHT CORN SYRUP

1/2 CUP HEAVY CREAM

8 TABLESPOONS (1/4 POUND)
UNSALTED BUTTER

3 CUPS TOASTED PECAN PIECES

To get rolling, first line a 9- by 5- by 3-inch loaf pan with plastic wrap. Then heat the sugar, corn syrup, cream, and butter in a 3-quart saucepan over medium-high heat; bring to a boil, stirring occasionally. Lower the heat and allow the mixture to simmer, stirring frequently, for 10 to 12 minutes until it achieves a light straw color. Add all of those crunchy pecan pieces and stir to combine. • Pour the mixture into the loaf pan, using a rubber spatula to spread it evenly. Refrigerate the nougat, uncovered, for 3 hours. Remove the nougat from the refrigerator and invert it onto a clean, dry cutting board, then remove and discard the plastic wrap. Use a serrated slicer to cut the nougat lengthwise into 4 (l-inch-wide) strips, and cut each strip into 8 (l-inch) squares. Wrap each square with plastic wrap and refrigerate until ready to enjoy. • What other riches can Nutty Nougat Nuggets bring besides eating them by the sticky handful? For a nutty treat, fold 1/4-inch pieces of nougat into semifrozen vanilla ice cream, then freeze until hard. Prepare to give your jaw a workout and look out for those gold fillings!

OAT BRAN CHEWS

Unless you eschew health news, make these gooey chews and get great reviews. Fortunately it doesn't take a poet or a prophet to prepare these divinely moist and toothsome snacks.

INGREDIENTS
(Yields 24 2-inch squares)

12 TABLESPOONS UNSALTED BUTTER

1 CUP HONEY

½ CUP TIGHTLY PACKED LIGHT BROWN SUGAR

2 CUPS OAT BRAN

2 CUPS QUICK COOKING OATS

1 TEASPOON BAKING SODA

2 CUPS RAISINS

1 CUP TOASTED WALNUT PIECES

First preheat the oven to 300 degrees Fahrenheit. Rather than waiting for a vision to appear while the oven comes to temperature, place the butter, honey, and brown sugar in the bowl of an electric mixer fitted with a paddle, beat on medium speed for 1 minute, then use a rubber spatula to scrape down the sides of the bowl. To this sticky mixture add the oat bran, quick oats, and baking soda; mix on low speed for 30 seconds. Now add the raisins and the walnut pieces, and mix on low speed for 1 minute until well combined.   •   Transfer the Oat Bran Chew mixture to a 9- by 13- by 2-inch nonstick rectangular cake pan and use the rubber spatula to spread it evenly. Bake in the preheated oven for about 45 minutes, until light brown. Remove from the oven and allow to cool to room temperature before cutting lengthwise into fourths, then make 5 crosswise cuts at 2-inch intervals. A wise cook will make lots of Oat Bran Chews for the next family outing.

P

MIDNIGHT PUDDING

**Anyone who makes this marvelously rich pudding deserves adulation.
This pudding is darkly chocolate yet so lightly textured that it literally dances on your spoon. And like the midnight sky speckled with stars,
the velvety darkness of the pudding lights up with surprising bits of white chocolate.**

INGREDIENTS
(Yields 4 servings)

4 OUNCES SEMISWEET CHOCOLATE, CHOPPED INTO 1/4-INCH PIECES

2 CUPS HALF-AND-HALF

1/2 CUP GRANULATED SUGAR

1/2 CUP UNSWEETENED COCOA

4 LARGE EGG YOLKS

1 TABLESPOON CORNSTARCH

4 OUNCES WHITE CHOCOLATE, CHOPPED INTO 1/8-INCH PIECES

Bring on the night by melting the semisweet chocolate in the top half of a double boiler over medium heat. Stir the chocolate constantly with a rubber spatula until it is completely melted and smooth, then remove from the heat and set aside. • Heat the half-and-half, 1/4 cup sugar, and the cocoa in a 3-quart saucepan over medium-high heat. When hot, whisk to dissolve the sugar. Bring to a boil. While the cream is heating, whisk the egg yolks, remaining sugar, and cornstarch in a medium bowl until slightly thickened and lemon-colored. Pour the boiling half-and-half mixture slowly into the egg yolks and stir to combine. Return the mixture to the saucepan and heat over medium-high heat, stirring constantly, until it begins to boil and becomes quite thick, about 30 seconds. Remove the pan from the heat and transfer the mixture to a large bowl. Add the melted chocolate, then place the bowl in ice water and stir the pudding until it is cold. Fold all but 2 tablespoons of chopped white chocolate into the pudding. Portion 3/4 cup of the pudding into each of 4 dessert dishes and sprinkle 1/2 tablespoon of the remaining white chocolate over the top of each. • Perhaps a devoted disciple will clean the saucepan in exchange for a sample of the pudding, leaving you free to enjoy the lusciously star-studded dessert. Sweet Dreams.

QUEEN OF QUINCE

QUINCE JAM TARTS

Once you smell the perfume emanating from your simmering saucepan of fresh quince, you'll know why quince has attained majestic status. This fragrant fruit simply must be cooked to be enjoyed. So waste no time jamming in the kitchen.

INGREDIENTS
(Yields 4 tarts)

1 1/2 CUPS ALL-PURPOSE FLOUR

1/2 CUP CHOPPED
TOASTED WALNUTS

1 TEASPOON MINCED
LEMON ZEST

8 TABLESPOONS (1/4 POUND)
BUTTER

4 LARGE QUINCE (OR 2 GRANNY
SMITH APPLES AND 2 PEARS)

1 CUP GRANULATED SUGAR

ICE CREAM (OPTIONAL)

First preheat the oven to 375 degrees Fahrenheit. Combine the flour, walnuts, and lemon zest in a medium-size bowl. Add the butter, then use your hands to mix the ingredients until crumbly and thoroughly combined. Place 1/2 cup of crumbs in each of 4 (4 1/2-inch-diameter and l-inch-deep) round, solid-bottomed, plain-sided tartlette molds. Use your hands to press the mixture evenly onto the bottom and sides of each mold. Place the molds on a baking sheet and set aside while preparing the quince jam. • Peel, core, and chop the quince into 1/2-inch pieces. Heat the quince and the sugar in a 3-quart saucepan over medium heat, stirring frequently to dissolve the sugar. Bring to a boil, then adjust the heat and allow to simmer, stirring frequently, for 20 minutes until the mixture is quite thick and your kitchen is completely perfumed. Remove the quince jam from the heat and divide the jam equally among the crumb crust-lined tartlette molds. Sprinkle the remaining crumb crust mixture, 1/4 cup per tart, over the jam in each mold. • Bake the tarts in the center of the oven for 30 minutes until bubbly and lightly browned. Remove from the oven. These tarts are at their best when served warm or at room temperature. Need something cool to accompany? Serve what all your subjects scream for—ice cream.

ROYAL RED RASPBERRY GRUNT

**Call it a grunt, slump, cobbler, crisp, buckle, crumble, or betty, these old-fashioned desserts with odd names sound "low-brow," but are fit for royalty.
They all have an abundance of cooked fruit, most have no bottom (crust that is), and whether the topping is tender, crisp, or crumbly, the total result is always scrumptious.**

INGREDIENTS
(Yields 8 servings)

1 1/2 CUPS ALL-PURPOSE FLOUR

1/4 CUP GRANULATED SUGAR

1 TABLESPOON MINCED ORANGE ZEST

2 TEASPOONS BAKING POWDER

4 TABLESPOONS UNSALTED BUTTER

1 CUP HEAVY CREAM

1 1/2 PINTS FRESHLY PICKED RED RASPBERRIES

WHIPPED CREAM OR VANILLA ICE CREAM (OPTIONAL)

Get this classic dessert underway first by preheating the oven to 375 degrees Fahrenheit. Place the flour, sugar, orange zest, and baking powder in a large bowl; stir to combine. Add the butter and stir with a fork until it is "cut into" the flour mixture. Add the cream and stir until smooth. • Randomly spoon the batter in heaping tablespoons into a 9- by 13- by 2-inch nonstick rectangular cake pan (do not spread the batter evenly as it will expand and come together while baking). Sprinkle the raspberries over the batter and bake in the preheated oven for 25 minutes until lightly browned. • Remove the grunt from the oven and allow it to stand for 5 minutes before cutting (notice how regal the berries appear perched on top of the baked batter). Cut the grunt lengthwise down the middle, then cut each half into 4 equal squares. Serve warm with whipped cream or with a colossal dome of vanilla ice cream and be prepared for many loyal subjects.

SESAME SHORTBREAD COOKIES

Open the kitchen door! If you don't, the troops will tear it down once they hear of the booty that beckons from within.

INGREDIENTS
(Yields 2 dozen cookies)

16 TABLESPOONS (¹/₂ POUND) UNSALTED BUTTER

¹/₂ CUP TIGHTLY PACKED LIGHT BROWN SUGAR

1 TEASPOON LIGHT SESAME OIL

2 CUPS ALL-PURPOSE FLOUR

¹/₂ CUP TOASTED SESAME SEEDS

Prepare for the onslaught first by preheating the oven to 300 degrees Fahrenheit. Place the butter, sugar, and sesame oil in the bowl of an electric mixer fitted with a paddle. Beat on medium speed for 2 minutes. Use a rubber spatula to scrape down the sides of the bowl, then beat on high for 30 seconds. Operate the mixer on low speed while carefully adding the flour; mix for 1 minute. Remove the bowl from the mixer and use a rubber spatula to finish mixing the dough until thoroughly combined. Wrap the dough with plastic wrap, then roll the dough on a flat surface to form a cylinder 6 inches long and 3 inches in diameter. Refrigerate the cylinder for 2 hours. • Remove the dough from the refrigerator and discard the plastic wrap. Cut the dough into 12 individual ¹/₂-inch-thick slices, then cut each slice in half to form a half-moon shape. Dip each half-moon into the sesame seeds, coating both sides and gently patting to allow the seeds to adhere to the dough. Transfer the half-moon shapes to 2 nonstick baking sheets and bake in the center of the oven for 20 to 22 minutes until lightly browned.

• Remove the cookies from the oven and allow them to cool to room temperature. Store the cookies in a tightly sealed plastic container for several days at room temperature or for several weeks in the freezer. But why in the world would you want to do that? Instead, line up your restless subjects, hand them a glass of milk and some shortbread half-moons, and don't worry about storing any cookies.

WHITE CHOCOLATE TRUFFLES

**Don't confuse these mellifluous morsels with the fungus called "truffle" that is rooted up by pigs.
Here's a white chocolate truffle so creamy and sublime that it is always
greedily devoured by humans. The only act more seductive than eating a chocolate truffle is
preparing them so that you can tempt others.**

INGREDIENTS
(Yields 2½ dozen truffles)

¾ CUP HEAVY CREAM

1 POUND WHITE CHOCOLATE,
CHOPPED INTO ¼-INCH PIECES

3 TABLESPOONS CONFECTIONERS'
SUGAR

2 TABLESPOONS UNSWEETENED
COCOA

Start by heating the cream in a 1½-quart saucepan over medium-high heat; bring to a boil. Place the chopped chocolate in a medium-size bowl, pour the boiling cream over, and allow it to stand, undisturbed, for 5 minutes. Gently stir with a whisk, transforming the mixture from lumpy and muddy to brilliant and smooth. Place the bowl, uncovered, in the refrigerator for 2 hours. • Line a baking sheet with parchment paper. Portion 30 level tablespoons of the chilled white chocolate mixture onto the parchment paper, and refrigerate for 15 minutes. • Combine the sugar and cocoa in a medium-size bowl. One at a time, roll the chocolate portions in your palms in a gentle circular motion, using just enough pressure to form smooth rounds. Roll the rounds in the sugar and cocoa mixture. Store the truffles in a tightly covered container in the refrigerator for up to a week. Take the truffles out of the refrigerator 30 minutes before luring the object of your desire.

UPSIDE-DOWN FROWN CAKE

Prepare to have your heart stolen by this winsome confection. Although the whimsical visage of this cake appears to frown, the first forkful is certain to elicit a smile.

INGREDIENTS
(Yields 6 to 8 servings)

1½ CUPS TIGHTLY PACKED LIGHT BROWN SUGAR

12 TABLESPOONS UNSALTED BUTTER

¼ POUND FRESH CHERRIES, PITTED AND CUT IN HALF

2 CUPS CHOPPED (¼-INCH PIECES) FRESH PINEAPPLE

1½ CUPS ALL-PURPOSE FLOUR

1 TEASPOON BAKING SODA

2 LARGE EGGS

½ CUP BUTTERMILK

WHIPPED CREAM (OPTIONAL)

Make haste! Preheat the oven to 350 degrees Fahrenheit. Place ½ cup brown sugar and 4 tablespoons of butter in the bowl of an electric mixer fitted with a paddle. Beat on medium speed for 2 minutes until, oh, so smooth. Transfer the mixture to a 10- by 1½-inch cake pan and use a rubber spatula to spread it evenly to the edges. Now for some fun—form a face with two eyes, a nose, and a frowning mouth by arranging the cherries cut side down in the mixture. Press gently to set the cherries in place. Fill the spaces around the cherries with the chopped pineapple and set the pan aside.

• Sift together the flour and baking soda onto wax paper. Place the remaining 1 cup brown sugar and 8 tablespoons butter in the bowl of an electric mixer fitted with a paddle. Beat on medium speed for 2 minutes. Add the eggs and beat once again on medium speed for 2 minutes. Use a rubber spatula to scrape down the sides of the bowl. Beat on high speed for 2 minutes, then add the sifted dry ingredients and the buttermilk, and mix on low speed for 30 seconds. Remove the bowl from the mixer and use a rubber spatula to finish mixing the batter until smooth. Pour the batter into the cake pan and spread evenly. Bake the cake in the center of the oven for 40 to 42 minutes until a toothpick inserted in the center comes out clean.

• Remove the cake from the oven and invert it onto a large plate—do *not* remove the pan. Allow the cake to stand at room temperature, with the pan on it, for 15 minutes. Remove the pan. Present the whole cake to your guests before slicing and serving warm with unsweetened whipped cream. Are you smiling yet?

VANILLA PUDDING DIPPERS

A bowl of pudding and a few pudding dippers will free the most earnest souls from the reality of life's restrictions. But before you indulge, you must do a little work.

INGREDIENTS
(Yields 32 dippers)

1 VANILLA BEAN

½ CUP GRANULATED SUGAR

8 TABLESPOONS (¼ POUND) UNSALTED BUTTER

1 LARGE EGG

2 CUPS ALL-PURPOSE FLOUR

Commence the preparation of the dippers by preheating the oven to 350 degrees Fahrenheit. Use a sharp paring knife to cut the vanilla bean in half lengthwise. Now use the back of the knife to scrape the seeds from the bean pod (discard the pod halves or use them to perfume a bowl of sugar). Place the seeds, sugar, and butter in the bowl of an electric mixer fitted with a paddle and beat on medium speed for 2 minutes. Add the egg, beat on medium for 1 minute, then use a rubber spatula to scrape down the sides of the bowl. Increase the speed to high and beat for 1 minute. Add the flour and mix on low speed for 30 seconds. Remove the bowl from the mixer and use a rubber spatula to finish mixing the dough until thoroughly combined. Wrap the dough with plastic wrap and refrigerate for 1 hour. • Remove the chilled dough from the refrigerator, discard the plastic wrap, and divide the dough into 32 heaping-teaspoon-sized pieces. Roll each portion of dough into a 3-inch strip. Place the strips, evenly spaced, onto 3 nonstick baking sheets, and use your fingers to flatten each strip to form paddle-style "dippers." Bake the dippers in the oven for 10 minutes until lightly browned. Remove from the oven and cool to room temperature. • What's next? Waste no time in making pudding, because as soon as these dippers cool, it will be time for delicious fun.

MUCHO MACHO MOCHA CREAM

There is no conflict in the alliance of coffee and chocolate. Indeed, these two flavors work together to capture and enrapture the palate.
In this recipe, assertive espresso combines with intense cocoa and raises the ante.

INGREDIENTS
(Yields 4 cups)

2 CUPS HEAVY CREAM

4 TABLESPOONS GRANULATED SUGAR

1 TABLESPOON INSTANT ESPRESSO POWDER

1 TABLESPOON UNSWEETENED COCOA

Before you charge, first place all the ingredients in the well-chilled bowl of an electric mixer fitted with a well-chilled balloon whip. Whisk on medium to dissolve the sugar, espresso powder, and cocoa, about 1 minute. Boost the speed to high and beat until thick and billowy clouds of cream are formed, about 45 seconds. Use the Mucho Macho Mocha Cream to embellish an ice cream sundae, ice a cake, or even to top cups of hot cocoa. To prevent the troops from sparring, you may want to double up on this remarkably simple recipe.

X-RATED

CHOCOLATE MINT X X X'S (KISSES)

These kisses are for all lovers, although experience may be helpful to seduce the bearer to share the candies.

INGREDIENTS
(Yields 24 kisses)

8 OUNCES SEMISWEET CHOCOLATE, CHOPPED INTO 1/4-INCH PIECES

2 OUNCES UNSWEETENED CHOCOLATE, CHOPPED INTO 1/4-INCH PIECES

3/4 CUP HEAVY CREAM

2 TABLESPOONS GRANULATED SUGAR

2 TABLESPOONS CHOPPED FRESH MINT

24 LARGE MINT LEAVES

The fantasy begins by placing the chopped chocolates in a medium-size bowl. Heat the cream, sugar, and chopped mint in a 1½-quart saucepan over medium-high heat, stirring to dissolve the sugar; bring to a boil. Immediately pour the boiling cream through a medium-gauge strainer into the bowl of chopped chocolate. Discard the mint. Use a whisk to gently stir until the cream and chocolate come together in a smooth and glistening pool. Pour the mixture onto a baking sheet with sides and use a rubber spatula to spread the chocolate to the edges. Refrigerate for 40 minutes.

• Remove the chocolate mint mixture from the refrigerator and transfer it to a pastry bag fitted with a medium star tip. Line a clean baking sheet with parchment paper. Arrange the mint leaves on the baking sheet. Form the kisses by piping about 1 tablespoon of chocolate mint mixture onto each leaf, creating a spiral conical shape, about 1 inch high for each kiss. Refrigerate the kisses for 30 minutes until firm. Store the kisses, tightly covered, in the refrigerator for up to a week. To steal a Kiss, deftly pluck the delicious morsel from the mint leaf with your lips. How'd you make out?

BERRY BERRY FROZEN YOGURT

**No twisting and turning necessary for the preparation of this stunningly colored frozen yogurt.
Just crank up the ice cream maker.**

INGREDIENTS
(Yields 1¾ quarts)

1 PINT BLUEBERRIES, STEMMED
AND WASHED

1 PINT STRAWBERRIES, STEMMED

¾ CUP GRANULATED SUGAR

½ PINT RED RASPBERRIES

4 CUPS PLAIN LOW-FAT YOGURT

First, heat the blueberries, strawberries, and sugar in a 3-quart saucepan over medium heat, stirring frequently to dissolve the sugar. Allow the berries to liquefy and begin to boil, then continue to cook, stirring often, for 10 minutes. Remove the mixture from the heat and stir in the raspberries. Place the pan in ice water and stir constantly until the mixture is cold (the lovely aroma of the berry purée makes this a pleasant task). • Stir the berry mixture into the yogurt, then freeze in an ice cream freezer following the manufacturer's instructions. Transfer the semifrozen yogurt to a plastic container. Securely cover the container, then place in the freezer for several hours before serving. • Your mantra should be "eat now," since the yogurt will get extremely hard the longer it stays in the freezer. If you are so disciplined to keep it, place the container of frozen yogurt in the refrigerator for about an hour before serving, and it will be mystically malleable.

Z

ZOMBIE OF ZABAGLIONE

"WHINE-FREE" LEMON ZABAGLIONE

**This warm and frothy custard will bring anyone back to life.
Zabaglione is an exceptionally satisfying dessert that comes to us by way of Italy.
Traditionally made with Marsala wine, this version
substitutes tangy fresh lemon juice for a "whine-free" experience.**

INGREDIENTS
(Yields 4 (1/2 -cup) servings)

4 LARGE EGG YOLKS

1/2 CUP GRANULATED SUGAR

1/2 CUP FRESH LEMON JUICE

1 TEASPOON MINCED
LEMON ZEST

Heat 1 inch of water to a simmer in a 3-quart saucepan. Place the egg yolks and sugar in a medium-size stainless steel bowl, and whisk vigorously to combine; add the lemon juice and zest, and whisk to combine. You should have a little life left in you for the next step. Place the bowl over the simmering water in the saucepan, then vigorously whisk the mixture in the bowl for about 8 minutes until thickened, but light and foamy. (You can use a hand-held electric mixer.) Immediately enjoy the Lemon Zabaglione with no further adornment, or portion the warm foam into dessert dishes filled with fresh fruit and nuts. *Evviva Zabaglione!*

AN ALPHABET OF SWEETS
RECIPES